*THE EF*
*EARLY INTERVENTIONS*

## PERSPECTIVES ON EDUCATION POLICY

**Institute of Education**
UNIVERSITY OF LONDON

# The Effectiveness of
# Early Interventions

## CHRISTINE OLIVER AND
## MARJORIE SMITH

© Institute of Education University of London 2000


Institute of Education University of London,
20 Bedford Way, London WC1H 0AL
Tel: 020 7612 6000  Fax: 020 7612 6126
www.ioe.ac.uk

*Pursuing Excellence in Education*


British Library Cataloguing in Publication Data:
a catalogue record for this publication is available
from the British Library

ISBN  0-85473-613-1

Produced in Great Britain by
Reprographic Services
Institute of Education University of London

Printed by Formara Limited
16 The Candlemakers, Temple Farm Industrial
Estate, Southend on Sea, Essex SS2 5RX


I1/0010-PEP No10-0900 (JR)

# CONTENTS

## ACKNOWLEDGEMENTS

This is a revised version of an invited paper presented at the second UK Government Cross-Departmental Review Seminar on Provision for Young Children which took place at the National Children's Bureau in London, in February, 1998. An earlier version of this paper was published in *Comprehensive Spending Review: Cross departmental review of provision for young children* – supporting papers, volume 1. HM Treasury July 1998.

We would like to thank Sandy Barker for her help in the preparation of this review.

# FOREWORD

This latest publication in the *Perspectives on Education Policy* series, by Marjorie Smith and Christine Oliver, reviews the research evidence on what works in early childhood interventions – in education, the family and the community – to combat subsequent educational failure and social exclusion.

The monograph is based on work for HM Treasury that has already informed the development of multi-agency initiatives such as Sure Start. However, its appearance now as a more public document is timely, as debates rage about the starting age for formal schooling and appropriate styles of early childhood education. Refreshingly, the authors do not take a doctrinaire position on such issues, but draw carefully on research from the UK and elsewhere to establish some general principles for effective interventions. The monograph includes a useful appendix on the character and outcomes of some specific interventions.

What is clear from this helpful review is that interventions that do not recognize and respond to the social context of provision, including specific local and family needs, are unlikely to be successful. Furthermore, it suggests to me that later phases of education may have much to learn from research on early interventions. However, it also shows that it must never be assumed that approaches that are effective in one context or phase will necessarily work well in another.

**PROFESSOR GEOFF WHITTY**
Director, Institute of Education

# 1
# Introduction

This review was originally commissioned for the Cross-Departmental Review of Provision for Young Children, in early 1998. As part of this, HM Treasury organized three seminars and commissioned a number of papers to inform the review process. The outcome of the Cross-Departmental Review was the announcement of Sure Start in the summer of 1998. Sure Start aims 'to work with parents and children to promote the physical, intellectual and social development of pre-school children – particularly those who are disadvantaged – to ensure that they are ready to thrive when they get to school'. The conception of Sure Start was evidence based, and it was planned from an understanding of the types of intervention, and characteristics of interventions, that have been demonstrated to be effective. There are clear objectives and targets specified, and these will be assessed both locally and by means of a national evaluation to establish whether Sure Start is successful in achieving its aims and objectives. It is intended, within a three-year period, to set up 250 Sure Start programmes across England as part of the drive to tackle child poverty and social exclusion. The first programmes were launched in early 1999, and became operational later that year.

## THE SCOPE OF THIS REVIEW

This review was intended not to describe the range and variety of early interventions, but rather aimed to assess the research evidence on what types of early interventions were most effective. The focus was on the characteristics of interventions that had been demonstrated to be effective in preventing social exclusion outcomes, in particular, poor educational outcomes, but also including where relevant, contact with the criminal justice system, teenage pregnancy, and failure in the labour market.

A considerable body of research exists in the UK and in other countries (particularly in the USA and Europe) examining the effectiveness of early interventions in the lives of young children (Farran, 1990; Halpern, 1990; Meisels and Shonkoff, 1990; Sylva and Wiltshire, 1993; McDonald and Roberts, 1995; Rutter, 1995; Guralnick, 1997). Published research in this field describes a wide range of problems experienced by different groups of children, such as the developmental needs of disabled children, the emotional and behavioural difficulties of looked after children, and the health and educational problems of children from socially disadvantaged backgrounds. The explicit focus of this literature is therefore upon children 'in need', and particularly those living in poverty, rather than children as a general social category. An implicit assumption underpinning such research is that something can and should be done to improve the life chances of children in such circumstances.

The logical corollary to this analysis of the 'problem' within a context of limited public resources tends to support a targeted approach, aimed at reducing the poor outcomes for children (such as poor health, low educational attainment and unemployment) which result from social inequality (Kumar, 1993). While this approach may make fiscal sense, it may also have unforeseen consequences, particularly for those perceived to be most 'in need'. It is commonly argued that, in order to avoid stigmatizing particular families, universal services which support children and families should be set up. The polarization of positions which occurs around this debate may obscure the range of options available and which we aim to present as a possible way forward.

## *Defining terms*

Before describing some examples of 'early interventions', it is necessary to set some boundaries to the scope of our review. By the term 'early' we mean during the early years which, for the purposes of this research includes infants and children up to the age of seven. We define 'interventions' as the implementation of an experimental project or programme, or a change in the focus or delivery of existing services. A decision was taken to focus on specific interventions and not on the efficacy of 'statutory' or whole provision or services, such as health visitors, day care or nursery education – but this has not been a clear-cut exclusion as there are some comments on the characteristics of effective 'statutory' services and provision.

In discussing the successes and failures of early interventions, we have included examples which use rigorous experimental designs and have measurable outcomes, as well as those which are more suggestive of effectiveness but may not have been fully evaluated. Interventions in this latter category are therefore presented as 'promising' rather than definitely 'effective'.

Although some of these 'interventions' take place within a single service (such as education), others show how important the concept of 'partnership' has become in the delivery of services. In practice, 'partnership' may have many different meanings and may operate on a variety of levels. A partnership may exist between parents and schools, for example, or between voluntary sector projects and statutory services. Sometimes partnerships are developed across different services, such as health, education and social services.

There is also the question of what is meant by 'effectiveness'. Different value systems will mean that individuals have different interpretations of effectiveness, and we discuss its potential meanings from a variety of standpoints and perspectives in the third section of this paper. Briefly, in the current context an effective intervention has been interpreted as one that acts to enhance performance or outcomes at school, and may have a measurable impact on later life – in practice this latter is rarely assessed. There are some notable exceptions, such as Alderson's study (1996) on children's perspectives on effective schools, and forthcoming research by Stevenson, Sonuga-Barke and Thompson (1999) on parenting strategies, but in the main one of the most striking features of the published literature in this field is the lack of evidence of effectiveness from the perspectives of parents and children. It is also notable that only a minority of 'interventions' target children's lives as separate from the family. The parental relationship, parenting styles and maternal health are among the key intervening variables which have been targeted as a mechanism for improving children's life chances.

Thus far our working definition of 'early interventions' has an implicit service orientation. There are clearly a great many ways in which interventions could be grouped and categorized. In support of the belief that children and families are best served if they are regarded in a holistic way, we have chosen to categorize and analyse the wide variety of interventions by looking at *who or what* is the central focus of the intervention. We have looked, for example, at whether an intervention is targeted primarily at the child, or the family, or the local environment. Some of the interventions we have described target more than one level, and indeed much research indicates that interventions are most effective if they target more than one level at a time (Guralnick, 1997).

We are also mindful that local conditions and problems interact in complex ways with national policies and structural factors such as changes in the labour market (Brannen and O'Brien, 1996; Brannen *et al.*, 1997). While this paper focuses upon localized initiatives, we are also aware that their capacity to produce positive outcomes for children and parents is influenced by the 'permitting circumstances' (Rutter, 1974) which governments have the power to shape at a national level.

Before discussing some examples of early interventions in more detail, the evidence relating to risk and protective factors in relation to educational outcomes is briefly reviewed, as are some important considerations which provide a context for analysing successes and failures in early intervention.

# 2
# Risk and protective factors

It is not proposed to discuss in any detail the risk factors for poor educational outcome in children, as these have been reviewed elsewhere (Pugh, 1998; Bynner, 1998). It is relevant, however, to acknowledge that there is considerable overlap between the risk factors predicting later antisocial behaviour and those predicting poor educational outcomes (McGee *et al.*, 1988; Farrington, 1995; Maughan *et al.*, 1996). These risk factors include material factors such as poverty and poor housing; family factors such as poor parenting (including neglect, abuse, harsh and inconsistent discipline, lack of supervision and marital conflict); and child factors, such as low intelligence and behaviour problems. Although not so immediately relevant to young children, school factors, such as early poor school performance and persistent truancy are also important predictors of later poor educational outcomes. While there is probably no practical distinction for pre-school children between the risk factors associated with later antisocial behaviour and those associated with poor educational outcomes (outcomes which themselves are highly correlated, particularly in boys), for young school-age children it has been suggested that behavioural difficulties such as high levels of impulsiveness and hyperactivity may best predict antisocial disorders, while reading difficulties may best predict poor educational outcomes (Bynner, 1998).

Data linking educational outcomes to familial factors is somewhat sparse. Using data from the British Household Panel study, Ermisch and Francesconi (1997) showed that mothers' educational status was a powerful predictor of children's educational outcomes, especially for girls. The effects of being raised in a single parent family had little effect on girls, but rather more on boys, but it was recognized that, 'part, if not all, of this negative effect of experience in a lone parent family reflects fewer economic resources in such families'. Gregg and Machin (1998) found from their analysis of the National Child Development Study (NCDS), that staying on at school was best predicted by mothers' and fathers' educational achievement, and by earlier performance on tests at age seven years. Parental relationship history (never having been in a lone parent family), unemployment and financial difficulties were also significant factors. Robertson and Symons (1996) looked at progress in reading and mathematics made by seven–11 year old children and found that parents' class and educational background were paramount. Robinson (1997) argues that the crucial intervening variable that has been measured in the cohort studies is that of parental interest in education, and this may go some way towards explaining the social class differences. It is clear that in terms of the identified risk factors for education achievement, home and family variables predominate over school or wider environmental factors. Bynner and Steedman (1995) say, 'the effects of economic disadvantage are so dominant in impeding basic skills development that they overwhelm the 'fine tuning' represented by school organization and curriculum'.

It is important to remember that risk factors are variables that have been identified as statistically associated with later poor outcomes, and are not necessarily causally associated with the outcome. The concept of proximal and distal variables can be useful in identifying what Logan and Spencer (1996) call chains of causal events. Distal variables tend to be demographic variables that are reasonably easy to measure, and describe major attributes, such as income, marital status, or age of the mother. It is difficult to propose a mechanism to demonstrate how any of these variables *per se* can impact on child outcome. But these variables through chains of causal events, predict other variables. For example, the break up of a marital relationship may be associated with considerable and continuing conflict, which may be a cause of stress to the mother, and may impact on her mental health and ability to parent. A low income may impact in a number of ways, as a stressor to the parents, and therefore on their ability to parent, and more directly it may mean that buying toys and books for children is not a priority. The relationship can be demonstrated between the number of children's books in the home, or the frequency children are read to, and children's reading ability. These variables, which tend to be more difficult to measure, are proximal variables. Other identified risk factors may not be causally implicated at all, but may simply be acting a markers for different variables that are implicated.

An understanding of the causal mechanisms underlying differences in outcomes is relevant to any intervention, as the proximal variables, rather than any distal or marker variables, are, or should be, the focus of the intervention if it is to succeed in achieving change. It is clear from the available research data that variables relating to family functioning, rather than family structure, are better predictors of child outcome (McFarlane, Bellissimo and Norman, 1995). It has been demonstrated, for example, that relationship conflict, which may both precede and continue after a marital break-up, is a stronger predictor of child outcome than divorce (Amato and Keith, 1991).

Much of the research on family functioning has investigated the extreme of poor parenting, in terms of child abuse, but it has been suggested that this research has much to offer towards an understanding of the determinants of individual differences in parenting (Belsky and Vondra, 1989). Belsky and Vondra and others place emphasis on multiple determinants of parenting. Their ecological model identifies 'multiple pathways by which individual (parental personality or child characteristics), historical (parental developmental history), and social (marital satisfaction and social network support), as well as circumstantial factors (poverty, job dissatisfaction, ignorance about child development) combine to shape parental functioning' (Belsky and Vondra, 1989: 157).

Three sources of influence on parental functioning were examined: the personality/psychological well-being of the parents, the characteristics of the child, and contextual sources of stress and support. The ability of parents to be sensitively attuned to their children was viewed as more likely if they were mature, psychologically healthy adults. The authors cited research suggesting that younger mothers, for example, have less realistic expectations for infant development than do older mothers, and that they tend to be less responsive to their new-borns and to engage their infants in less verbal interaction. Other research has highlighted the importance of psychological maturity and personality attributes like self-esteem and locus of control as factors contributing to sensitive, nurturant parenting. Studies of parenting and psychological disturbance, such as psychosis and depression, have supported the view that an individual's personality can serve to either support or undermine parenting ability.

If parenting is construed as multiply determined, the determinants can be viewed as operating at different levels: factors associated with the family and the child's immediate environment; broader ecological or community systems which directly impact on the family; and the nature of modern culture and society (Drake and Pandey, 1996). At the distal end one can identify community norms, and the chronic lack of (community) resources in poor neighbourhoods, while more proximal influences include economic distress and isolation, social isolation, high levels of stress and a sense of negativism. Concepts of resilience or protective factors operate at the most proximal level, in terms of differences in individual reactions to stressors in the immediate family of wider environment. Belsky and Vondra identify three distinct sources of stress and support as likely to promote or undermine parental competence. The quality of the relationship between the parents, and social support, are known influences on parenting. A third contextual source of stress and support on parenting considered by Belsky and Vondra was that of employment, or lack of it. In addition to its deleterious effects on material standards of living, unemployment is likely to lead to additional strains on family relationships arising from lowered self-esteem, lack of an external routine, and so on.

Belsky and Vondra suggest that interactions between these three sources of influence mean that parenting can be viewed as a buffered system. The undermining effect of a difficult child, for example, may be lessened when the parent has plenty of personal psychological resources and social support. Conversely, an easy child could compensate for limited personal resources or for the lack of social support. Resilience, in terms of a good outcome for a child where risk factors are present, can result from the personal resources of the parent, buffering parental functioning, or from the personal resources of the child buffering against parental functioning.

Causal and mechanistic interpretations will determine, to some extent, the focus and timing of any intervention. For example, if the aim of an intervention is to improve reading skill in young children, and if the causes of early reading failure are thought to reside within the family and be the result of lack of early exposure to books and written material, the intervention is likely to be home-based and may focus on changing the behaviour of the mother with respect to the child. If on the other hand, early reading problems are viewed as the result of failure to acquire the basic skills, the intervention is likely to be later, school-based, and to focus on the child. These distinctions of focus explain some of the differences in approach, and may explain why some interventions have unexpected outcomes, and others do not work as anticipated. An intervention is only effective if it achieves its objectives. In designing an intervention it is important to identify the objectives clearly in terms of the causal processes or hypothesized processes, and the proposed mechanisms that the intervention aims to influence, and then build in an assessment to measure this.

# 3
# Setting the context

## RESEARCH METHODOLOGIES

A number of important caveats must be considered in relation to evaluating interventions in the lives of children. Essentially:

- very few interventions have been rigorously evaluated
- some evaluations fail to record unanticipated outcomes
- few evaluations are both longitudinal *and* scientifically rigorous
- some outcomes are difficult to measure
- information on processes can be as important as the measurement of outcomes
- evaluations need to take different perspectives and values into account

- small-scale, innovative projects rarely have the funds to evaluate their work.

Recent research syntheses have suggested that very few interventions have been rigorously evaluated using scientific methods such as randomized control trials (RCT) (Oakley, 1996; Alderson *et al.*, 1996). The RCT method helps to ensure that the effect of an intervention is accurately measured or attributed.

Additionally, some evaluations fail to record unanticipated outcomes. For example, Project Head Start, one of the best-known of these interventions, was initially described as a failure. Later research, however, using more rigorous methods and measuring longer term and wider social outcomes concluded that Head Start was indeed an example of an effective intervention (Smith and Bissell, 1970; McKey *et al.*, 1985).

Furthermore, few evaluations have been longitudinal *and* scientifically rigorous, particularly in the UK. Much of the longitudinal research that does exist in the UK focuses upon children's health (e.g. Blaxter, 1986; Kuh and Wadsworth, 1993). Information on how an intervention (or aspects of an intervention) during the early years can cause, or be associated, with positive or negative effects during teenage years and beyond is therefore limited. The most well-known longitudinal interventions originate in the US (for example, the Head Start findings and the evaluation of the Perry Pre-School Project).

In this country, birth cohort studies provide useful information on life trajectories and risk factors from the early years through to adulthood. While these are not interventions, the information adds to an understanding of the factors implicated in better or worse outcomes, and can for example be used to look at the effects of day care.

Despite these drawbacks, the wide range of published research in this field provides a reasonably sound basis upon which to draw lessons about 'what works' in the early years. Even research which is limited to measuring relatively short-term effects (e.g. over 3–5 years) can inform a discussion about the relative merits of different interventions and their outcomes for children.

There are other important reasons for not restricting our focus to only those interventions which have been evaluated according to 'gold standard' criteria. Some outcomes are difficult to measure (such as child self-esteem, for example) and research which produces measurable outcomes may not tell us very much about *how* outcomes were achieved. It is this process information which is often of particular interest to organizations seeking to replicate proven models of good practice.

Intervention 'success' or 'failure' cannot be separated from questions of perspective. Parents and children may have different views from the professionals they work with, and from researchers. Children in particular are rarely asked about their experiences or views about a particular 'intervention'. Qualitative studies carried out alongside more scientifically rigorous evaluations, can provide important additional information on the perceptions of different 'stakeholders'.

Further, many of the more innovative early interventions have originated in the voluntary sector. The value of such projects is that they have 'grass roots' origins and this provides a useful counterbalance to the dangers which may arise from the imposition of insensitive and inappropriate 'top down' interventions on unwilling families and communities. These projects operate on small budgets and are the least likely to have the resources for conducting sound evaluations of their work. There are also more pragmatic considerations to take into account: can we wait for more longitudinal, scientifically rigorous studies to be completed before we design more interventions, or do we know enough already? It is hoped that this review will go some way towards answering this question.

## SOCIAL AND POLITICAL CONTEXT

Much of the early literature on effective interventions originating in US during the 1960s and 1970s was motivated by governmental interest in ending 'cycles of deprivation' in which poor outcomes (poverty, low educational attainment, unemployment, poor housing, etc.) appeared to be passed down between generations. Pre-school education for poor and black families in urban areas was the focus of many of these early interventions (Schweinhart and Weikart, 1980; Lee, Brooks-Gunn and Schnur, 1988; Bailey, 1997).

Current governmental interest in securing better outcomes for children runs along similar lines. Although the language used in this debate has changed – for example, we now talk about 'risk factors' for 'social exclusion' – the target groups tend to be the same: poor families in inner urban communities. However, the structure of these households has changed considerably over the last 20 to 30 years, with single-parent households now more common (OPCS, 1994; Kiernan, Land and Lewis, 1998). There are also important structural changes in the labour market, with an increase in jobs requiring skills in new technology, while the number of manual jobs has declined. Consequently, jobs which once absorbed people with few educational qualifications are now less available. Resources have become more polarized between 'work rich' and 'work poor' households. There are therefore strong market-driven arguments for ensuring that society produces an educated work force. As changes in the labour force create greater risks for 'social exclusion', concern about the social and economic costs of delinquency and crime has also come more sharply into focus.

The gendered aspects of these two important themes – changes in family structures and patterns of criminal or delinquent behaviour – have received little attention. In practice, the undesirable consequences of social exclusion tend to focus upon the risk of delinquency and unemployment in males, and in females on the risk of teenage pregnancy, single parenthood and depression.

## DEVELOPMENTS IN POLICY AND PRACTICE

Alongside widespread public and governmental concern about changes to the 'traditional' family structure, a shift has occurred in the locus of 'intervention' from the child's development (cognitive and emotional) during pre-school years in educational settings, towards interventions which target parenting skills and knowledge. Parenting skills and styles are seen as one of the main intervening variables which mediate educational and social outcomes for children (Utting, 1995; Pugh, De'Ath and Smith, 1994). In recent years, there has been a steady growth in the number of projects and initiatives (many voluntary sector based) which aim to help parents in their task of parenting. The range of programmes is wide, and includes those which provide social support to parents, as well as those that aim to educate parents, or to train them in specific parenting skills, such as managing difficult behaviour. Within each of these types, which are not clear-cut divisions, programmes range along a dimension from those focused on the prevention of adverse outcomes (such as child injury or abuse) in high-risk populations, to those aiming to promote better parenting in volunteer population groups. In the UK, NEWPIN (Cox *et al.*, 1991; Pound, 1994) and Home-Start UK (Cox, 1993; Frost *et al.*, 1996) are both well established examples of social support interventions. PIPPIN is a well known example of a parent education programme. Parent-Link, developed by Parent

Network, Mellow Parenting (Puckering *et al.*, 1994) and the approach developed in the US by Webster-Stratton (Webster-Stratton, 1994; 1998), but now used by several groups in the UK (e.g. Scott, 2000), are all examples of programmes using the parenting skills based approach.

This shift, from the child at pre-school or primary school to the parents as the locus for intervention, is not put forward as a rigid separation. Services and policies with an educational component such as integrated early years centres continue to be developed for children. Family support provided by social services departments may also include a day care package for the child. But this latter intervention is often conceptualized at the level of family 'rescue', and serious concerns have been voiced about the quality of care and education offered to children in these services, and the effects of stigmatization upon the parents and children who use them.

Calls have been made for research which more directly informs practice issues (Guralnick, 1997; Utting, 1995). If social exclusion is viewed as the result of 'unmet needs', then it follows that the best way to tackle social exclusion is to 'meet needs'. A key question being asked is: which specific intervention can be demonstrated by research to match the needs of an individual child or family?

## VALUE SYSTEMS

The mechanisms and targets for 'early interventions' cannot easily be separated from the value systems which underpin them. Much uninformed social commentary locates social 'problems' in family structures and their breakdown rather than in wider social inequalities or the more specific characteristics of families which produce poor outcomes for children, such as persistent family conflict (Utting, 1995). It is important, therefore, for governments to think through both the motivation and the presentation of planned early interventions in order to avoid stigmatizing selected families and their children. This is both an ethical and practical point since interventions which place children and their parents within a deficit model may undermine levels of participation among those families that are most in need of support. Evidence suggests that self-esteem is an important ingredient in enabling families and children to survive and flourish, and a stigmatizing service is likely to undermine self-esteem (McGurk *et al.*, 1993).

The United Nations Declaration on the Rights of the Child offers a useful framework for shaping the values upon which interventions are made on behalf of children. These rights include adequate health, health care, standard of living, leisure and play activities, specialist support for disabled children, protection from abuse, and the right to be involved in decisions on matters which affect them. In order for this value framework to inform the nature of 'early interventions', recognition will, however, need to be made of the tension which had traditionally existed in British social policy between (a) seeing the child as the private responsibility of the family until a breakdown in the family system or failure to maintain acceptable standards of care occurs, and (b) regarding the role of social interventions as maximizing children's life chances by making a range of universal and targeted services available to families. A fundamental shift in focus is required if children's life chances are to be seen as both a community and governmental responsibility requiring the deployment and investment of national and local resources.

The value system which is adopted also needs to take into account aspects of social diversity. Interventions which are shaped taking into account the needs and wishes of local communities will have a greater chance of incorporating differences in perspective according to age, class, gender and ethnicity. The European Childcare Network's (1992) checklist for quality services for young children may be taken as a useful starting point in this respect. It suggests that children's services should be:

- accessible
- flexible
- according to family needs
- take into account parental views
- reflect the local community
- cost effective.

## DELIVERY MECHANISMS

Although this literature review does not focus on delivery mechanisms the question of effectiveness cannot be divorced from *how* an intervention is delivered and *by whom.* Research in the US has shown that multi-disciplinary work with local community involvement has some of the most beneficial outcomes for children (Guralnick, 1997). Services and projects which serve a local community are more accessible because they reduce transport costs, travelling and waiting times, which have been shown to be significant stressors on mothers (Mayall and Foster, 1989). However, approaching problems and delivering services in a child- or family-focused way presents challenges to service and agency divisions. Different services such as social services, housing, and education, see children and parents through different lenses and operate within different legislative frameworks (Petrie, 1994). Multi-agency delivery mechanisms also have not been sufficiently evaluated and there are indications that considerable time and energy may need to be put into breaking down professional and agency barriers in order to produce working and effective partnerships (Power, Whitty and Youdell, 1995).

## COST EFFECTIVENESS

A minority of early interventions in the lives of children have included any consideration of cost effectiveness (Holtermann, 1998; Welsh, 1997). Holtermann has outlined what would be required for interventions to be assessed from a cost effectiveness perspective, but also acknowledges that such a process implies a requirement to target resources where they are most needed, and in ways which will have the most effect (Holtermann, 1998). She also acknowledges that targeting resources at disadvantaged families can be potentially stigmatizing.

The debate about universal versus targeted services has also been aired in other fields, such as health education, where differences of view have arisen about the merits of targeting services and publicity towards 'at risk' groups. One of the risks of adopting a universal approach which does not acknowledge differences in resources and lifestyles, is that varieties and levels of 'need' become obscured. The groups at highest risk are also the most resistant to health education messages, and in the current context, the least likely to engage in interventions. It was notable that before the health education campaign aimed at reducing the risks of cot death in infants, proportionally more babies in the most disadvantaged group were sleeping on their backs, against prevailing advice. When this advice was changed, and a campaign was launched to encourage mothers to place babies on their backs to sleep, proportionally more of the babies of the most needy mothers were placed on their front to sleep (Conroy and Smith, 1999).

It could be argued that there is a case for a broad spectrum of interventions targeted at areas of deprivation. If these interventions were of a sufficiently high quality and acceptable to local people, they could assist in reducing social inequality without creating social stigma. Whatever approach is taken, it remains the case that there will be a small but highly significant group of families who will not easily be reached by either a universal or a targeted approach, unless special measures are taken to identify and engage them. This highly mobile population is likely to be the most needy.

A number of other factors relate to an analysis of the potential cost effectiveness of interventions. As longitudinal studies such as Perry Pre-School Project have shown, savings can appear many years after the original investment in the intervention (Berrueta-Clement et al., 1984). Some long-term outcomes may not be measured either because the evaluation does not examine long-term effects, or because of a less than comprehensive evaluation of all the possible outcomes. Benefits can also accrue to a wide range of public bodies and substantial benefits may not necessarily be made by the investing body. The distribution of costs and benefits resulting from interventions in the early years underlies the need for partnership at the budgetary as well as strategic level.

As Holtermann has pointed out, an assessment of cost cannot be divorced from effectiveness studies. In some cases, approximate cost benefit analyses can be made *post hoc* if sufficient information is provided on the processes involved in the intervention (such as staff time, numbers of service users) and if approximate estimates can be made of the total costs of a problem to society (e.g. youth crime).

One of the keys to achieving maximum benefit from any intervention is that it is acceptable to participants, and widely used (Oakley *et al.*, 1995). The acceptability of an intervention to target groups should therefore be an integral component of a thorough cost-benefit analysis. It makes good fiscal sense to design interventions which will be both accessible and appropriate from the perspective of both parents and children.

Some interventions result in outcomes which are difficult to measure. Whether a child thinks that her quality of life has been improved by the availability of a local play centre may be difficult to assess, laden as these assessments are with individual, family and social value systems.

# 4
# What Works and What Does Not Work?

Interventions in the lives of children can be grouped into tiers according to who, or what, is the main focus of the intervention. A table of tiers is shown on p.24.

In some cases, more than one family member may provide the focus for a multi-faceted intervention, or an intervention may be designed to operate at more than one level. The Seattle Social Development Programme (Hawkins *et al.*, 1992) for example, targeted both changes to the pre-school curricula and parent education. Other interventions, such as Home-Start, may provide parental support which includes an element of parent education. The Atlanta Project attempts to operate on the environmental, parental and child tiers.

As the family is usually the primary and immediate social context

# TIERS OF INTERVENTION

| TARGET | EXAMPLE OF INTERVENTION |
|---|---|
| a) the child | Pre-school provision for disadvantaged children |
| b) maternal health | Social support during pregnancy, counselling for depression, and health visiting |
| c) the parents/ child-in-the-family | *Informal*: e.g. parenting education, parental support (mentoring, self-help, open access family centres for advice and support) |
| | *Formal*: e.g. family centres (social services), day care services for 'at risk' children |
| d) local environment | Local community facilities, quality services (e.g. schools, affordable leisure facilities) housing design and child-friendly environment, employment opportunities |
| e) national context and policies | Tax and benefits system, government funding for services which support families and children |

for the child, parents are often the focus for achieving better outcomes for children. This is particularly the case for mothers with infants, where the mothers' own health and well-being may be targeted in order to improve outcomes for their children. Indeed, while the gender-neutral term 'parenting' may be desirable in some contexts, its use can also obscure the gendered character of many social interventions in the family. Although some parenting education classes may be open to both mothers and fathers, few interventions in the family directly target fathers as a way of relieving the burden of care upon the mother, or as a way of strengthening relationships between fathers and their children.

Although these interventions aim to improve outcomes for children in the immediate and sometimes long-term future, we do not have a good idea of what a genuinely child-centred intervention would look like. This would require a willingness to start with the child's needs and wishes.

We will now discuss examples of what has and what has not worked under each of these tiers of intervention. Further details of the evaluations of some of the interventions described below, are given in an appendix.

## a) Intervening in children's lives

### (I) PRE-SCHOOL INTERVENTIONS

Many of the interventions that have targeted children outside the family have taken the form of pre-school programmes to improve the cognitive and social development of disadvantaged children in deprived areas. The pre-school years are generally acknowledged as representing a crucial phase in the child's development. The importance of quality pre-school interventions is of particular benefit to children from poor backgrounds including those who are disadvantaged by inadequate parental care, or as a result of removal from parental care into local authority care. Research shows that even when children are removed from their family of origin into a long-term foster placement, the care they receive is rarely sufficient to close the developmental gap in terms of their educational attainment (Jackson, 1994). The educational needs of looked-after children are often overlooked.

The general consensus of research into the effects of pre-school programmes is that, if they are of high quality and have appropriate educational components, they lead to positive outcomes for children in the short- and long-term. These positive outcomes cover a wide range of variables, including educational attainment, pro-social behaviour, and employment prospects (Sylva and Wiltshire, 1993; Lazar and Darlington, 1982). Much has been written about the concept of quality within early years provision. As Pugh says, 'The issue of quality has been discussed in almost every book on early childhood services published in the last decade, and must be seen as a complex process rather than a set of tidy outcomes' (Pugh, 1996: 23). Pugh identifies three key issues: the provision of an appropriate curriculum, well-trained staff, and good relationships between staff and parents. Within this definition, it is clear that quality is not an absolute concept, but is both flexible in terms of what is appropriate in different circumstances, and interactive with different local needs. In their review of early childhood services, Mooney and Munton (1997) identified high-quality provision as providing consistency, stability, and sensitivity of care, which in turn was related to staff–child ratios, staff training, education and physical conditions.

We will make reference here to examples of two pre-school interventions (Head Start and Perry Pre-School) in the US because they are among the few longitudinal studies which have measured the impact of pre-school programmes upon the life trajectories of children. The data are sufficiently robust to enable the evaluators to claim that these pre-school programmes *caused* the more positive outcomes for the experimental children, as compared with children in the control groups.

## HEAD START

The initial results of evaluations on the Head Start programme were disappointing (Westinghouse Learning Corporation, 1969). Changes in children's IQ were measured as the yardstick for success and it was found that initial improvements in children who had participated in the Head Start programme were not sustained through primary school. It was only later that other broader measures of success were obtained, for example, educational attainment, anti-social behaviour, use of remedial educational services, and track records in employment and offending behaviour (McKey *et al.*, 1985). This example of the initial 'failure' of an intervention, but later success, illustrates the importance of measuring long-term outcomes, and ensuring that anticipated as well as unanticipated outcomes are assessed as part of the evaluation process.

## PERRY PRE-SCHOOL

The Perry Pre-School High/Scope intervention (Hohmann, Barnet and Weikart, 1979) in the US has also received wide attention, possibly because of its demonstrable long-term benefits, and cost effectiveness (Berrueta-Clement *et al.*, 1984) (see Appendix). It has been claimed that for every $1 invested by the state in this intervention, $7 was saved to society. It is further estimated that 65% of these savings from the Perry Pre-School Project were made by the criminal justice system. This intervention is an exception both in including an estimate of cost effectiveness, and in collecting information on long-term outcomes (Schweinhart, Barnes and Weikart, 1993). Evidence of cost effectiveness helped justify an argument for investment in pre-school services for disadvantaged children (Schweinhart and Weikart, 1980).

Compared with a control group, High/Scope children showed fewer behavioural difficulties, a lower drop out rate, higher levels of educational attainment, a lower teenage pregnancy rate, and had higher incomes and levels of home ownership in their adult lives. Perry Pre-School evaluators identified the causal chain behind these outcomes, with the experience of pre-school leading to greater commitment to learning, and subsequently to achievement.

The Perry Pre-School Project is also important because it was shown to be especially effective in improving the life prospects of poor black children, and therefore illustrates the value of pre-school experiences as providing 'added protection' against social disadvantage and discrimination. It also shows that an intervention which seeks to compensate for social inequality does not necessarily have to be stigmatizing and undermining of achievement (Schweinhart, Barnes and Weikart, 1993). The scheme was also shown to protect against the risk of delinquency and the need for special education.

*STYLES OF INTERVENTION*

There are other features of the Perry Pre-School programme which might help to explain its success. It was one of a number of pre-school interventions which sought to evaluate whether different outcomes could result from different styles of intervention. Its success was partly attributed to the *content* of the programme, which involved activities linked to themes and had a 'plan-do-review' approach to working with children as its central component. This means that each day children started by planning with their key worker what they were going to do for the day, and at the end of the day, after the activities, there was a small group session where they reviewed what they had done, how they had felt about it, as well as any difficulties they had encountered. The programme was highly task oriented, with a learning process style. Pre-school staff were described as developing a *dialogue* with children, which suggests that an adult-child relationship which is exploratory and supportive in nature leads to higher levels of self-esteem in children. The intervention was also characterized by high levels of parental participation. It has been shown in other research that parental interest in a child's education is a key factor influencing their cognitive development (Woodhead, 1985; Osborn and Millbank, 1987).

## CHILDREN'S PLAY AND ENJOYMENT

Similar studies have been undertaken in the UK comparing the content of different pre-school programmes. The research suggests that, in addition to exposing children to a range of learning experiences, the factor of children's enjoyment in producing positive outcomes cannot be ignored. The educative role of play during the early years is widely acknowledged (e.g. David, 1996). The success of High/Scope has been attributed to the role of adults who, rather than 'dominating' play, acted to provide a 'scaffolding' (Bruner, 1983), by giving encouragement, making suggestions, and using language to describe actions (Sylva, Smith and Moore, 1986). In a comparison of three pre-school models in the UK (one based on a High/Scope, one on 'free play' and one on a formal pre-school curriculum), the two play-based schemes were found to produce better outcomes for children. Children 'hothoused' in the curriculum-based scheme showed more behaviour problems and lack of commitment to school during primary years (Schweinhart, Weikart and Larner, 1986).

The importance of a child-centred approach was also illustrated in an early example of an effort to introduce the High/Scope model into the UK. In 1984–85, High/Scope was piloted in five pre-school centres in the UK. A before-and-after study conducted by the Nuffield Foundation involved 100 children who were observed a year after the High/Scope model was introduced. The research focused upon patterns of play, the extent and characteristics of interactions between adults and children, and between children (Sylva, Smith and Moore, 1986).

## REPLICATING MODELS OF GOOD PRACTICE

There are some important lessons about replication across social and cultural divides:

* models of good practice need to be sensitively adapted to take into account cultural differences
* models of pre-school intervention should be implemented flexibly to take account of the needs and wishes of different groups and individuals.

The importance of the pre-school in social learning as well as education should not be overlooked. In the case of the Nuffield study, staff resisted what they perceived to be an over-emphasis upon education and insufficient space for children to be child-like (that is, have the freedom to play) and to spend time interacting with other children. This suggests that the views and needs of staff and children are important factors to take into account both in the development and evaluation of interventions.

## (II) DAY CARE

Although day care is not generally classified as an 'intervention' in the lives of children, it has important preventive value as an adjunct to parental support. There is a lack of research on the role of nurseries in protecting children, but day care is commonly used by social services departments as a way of providing 'compensatory' care to children and protecting them from further harm (David, 1994; Statham, 1994).

Much of the debate in this country tends to be focused on the relative merits of different types of day care, and of the beneficial or detrimental outcomes for children and their parents (Jowett and Sylva, 1986). McGuire and Richman (1986) associated day care with low educational attainment and an increased level of behaviour problems during primary school, compared with children who attended playgroups. However, this study failed to take into account the fact that children in social services day care were more likely to have emotional problems before they entered day care.

As a result of the traditional professional divide between care and education, the educational benefits of day care are often overlooked (Sylva, Siraj-Blatchford and Johnson, 1992). Zoritch, Roberts and Oakley (1998) have conducted eight randomized controlled trials of outcomes for children in day care. All showed that day care had positive effects upon children's educational attainment.

There are numerous examples of services which attempt to bridge the divide between education and care (e.g. 'educare' services). The needs of working mothers have been reflected in the recent increase, within the private sector, in quality day care facilities that offer an active learning curriculum at the same time as extended hours. 'Educare' services offer innovative models of integrative and interdisciplinary working. However, inter-professional conflict is also often a feature of these models and, as in all partnership efforts, considerable energy and commitment is required to sustain them. One of the factors identified as an important feature of successful multi-agency centres is the presence of a strong, energetic and charismatic leader (Makins, 1997).

Although these interventions have rarely been longitudinal, cost benefit analyses have been undertaken. Barnett and Escobar (1990) compared a day care programme for disadvantaged families with a pre-school project with a language-based curriculum. They found that both the schemes were cost effective in terms of later savings in schooling and medical care

## QUALITY AND TYPE OF CARE

Melhuish and Moss (1991) have compared outcomes for children cared for in three different settings: at home with a parent, with childminders, and in a nursery. This study found that quality and continuity of care were more strongly associated with positive outcomes than type of care. Similar conclusions were reached in a recent review conducted by Mooney and Munton (1997). They found that despite the use of other pre-school services, family life continued to be the most important influence on young children's development, but the quality of childcare (rather than its type) was of key importance.

## FRAGMENTATION

Interventions in the range of pre-school services in the UK will need to take into account the historical legacy of a predominantly fragmented and partially compensatory pattern of provision. Pre-school nurseries and playgroups for children aged three provide a part-time service and tend to be used by a socially mixed group of children. Private day care has traditionally been used by working parents and the cost and quality of care varies. Economic necessity may force some parents into the choice between low-cost, low quality day care and employment. Day care run by social services is generally targeted at children 'at risk' and carries the danger of stigma and lowered self-esteem for children and their parents (McGurk *et al.*, 1993).

A more positive approach to early years services might promote pre-school services as a positive resource for parents according to varying needs and as a mechanism for promoting the well-being of children. In France, for example, pre-school services are provided in school premises, are of high quality and non-stigmatizing. They are funded by the state, local authorities and private sources. Even if a universal pre-school service could not be resourced, schools provide a valuable community resource which could be built upon in order to support children and their parents, particularly in deprived areas.

## (III) PRIMARY SCHOOLS

Children from poor backgrounds are at a significant disadvantage during the early years of primary school. Lack of resources and opportunities for engaging in learning in the home caused by inadequate play materials and parental involvement, for example, place children at an educational disadvantage. The role of primary school teachers in this context is to try to close this gap in skills and resources. It is worth quoting the findings of a recent study by Hurry and Sylva (1997) here:

We suggest that children who are total non-readers, and those who come from impoverished homes find it difficult to benefit fully from ordinary school instruction. Children with some literacy skills, or from better off homes, are more able to cope in the classroom ... their difficulties (i.e. those of the impoverished) may be related to lack of materials and/or literacy activities in the home.

Low educational achievement associated with early reading

difficulties and difficulty settling to educational tasks have been shown to be significant risk factors in relation to anti-social behaviour. Thus schools have been seen as one arena where interventions can bring about improved outcomes for children. Rutter *et al.* (1979) have pointed to the value of schools in supporting home–school relations, and in promoting an ethos of mutual support between pupils which may help to discourage bullying. Interventions have also been designed at the level of the curriculum. One approach has been to boost young children's reading skills, as in the Reading Recovery Programme (Clay, 1991).

Evaluation studies of interventions with older children who experienced problems learning to read have rarely found any lasting improvements (Maughan, Gray and Rutter, 1985). There has therefore been a shift in emphasis to targeting interventions at children during their first few years of primary school. The Reading Recovery programme (see Appendix) which was developed in New Zealand (Clay, 1979) has been shown to be effective in raising reading standards.

A recent study by Hurry and Sylva (1997) compared the effects of two different approaches to improving reading skills. At first follow up, the children in the Reading Recovery intervention group had made substantially more progress than children in control groups on all measures of reading and writing. Although training in particular skills was reflected in differences in these component skills, there was no measurable overall effect on reading. In the longer term follow up, although both intervention groups were somewhat ahead of their within-school controls, the intervention effects were small. When the analysis was concentrated on the most deprived children, the original advantage of reading recovery in both reading and spelling reappeared. In terms of cost effectiveness, Reading Recovery was found to be costly but no more so than standard approaches to educating children with reading difficulties in schools.

The Seattle Social Development Project (Hawkins *et al.*, 1992) is also a useful example of a two-pronged approach to improving children's educational attainment and reducing anti-social behaviour during the early years of primary school, by involving both parents and teachers. The programme combined a parent education programme which taught skills in dealing with difficult behaviour and reinforcing pro-social behaviour. Parents were also encouraged to show an interest in their child's education. Teachers were trained in behaviour management and communication skills, particularly in relation to conflict resolution. They were also trained to deliver a problem-solving curriculum. The project was evaluated and shown to have positive outcomes for children, particularly in relation to increased attainment and a reduction in anti-social behaviour. Over the longer term, the experimental group were shown to have lower levels of criminal convictions, and lower levels of teenage pregnancy (Communities That Care, 1996).

## (IV) MOTHERS AS EDUCATORS

Despite ample evidence of the importance of the mother in the early development of the child (Tizard and Hughes, 1984), relatively few evaluated interventions focus on the mother as an educator of the child during the early years. Research has shown that the child's cognitive development is influenced by the mother's level of education and that an intervention targeted at supporting the mother in this role can have positive outcomes for children. Involving parents to help with children's reading in the early school years has been shown to be effective in improving reading outcomes and, in changing parents' attitudes towards schools, produced other unexpected positive outcomes (Tizard, Schofield and Hewison, 1982).

The Mother and Child Verbal Interaction Project is the rather ungainly title for a home-based intervention which has had positive outcomes for children (described in Communities That Care, 1996). This project targeted low income single mothers who had a low level of education. 'Toy demonstrators' paid weekly visits to the home in order to support the mothers in playing with their children. At the end of the programme, families were allowed to keep the toys. This initiative was shown to have long-term positive effects measured by achievement and IQ tests at 5th and 8th grades. An unforeseen benefit was that positive outcomes were also shown for siblings. This was attributed to the mother having generalized her skills to other siblings in the family.

## b) Intervening in parents' lives

In practice, the large majority of interventions involving parents are focused on the main caretaker, who in most cases is the mother. As discussed earlier few interventions involve fathers in any capacity, and even fewer are designed for fathers.

### (I) MOTHERS

Many of the interventions that have targeted mothers have worked within a social stress model, and have been concerned with preventing postnatal depression or alleviating its effects. Other studies have focused on training mothers to interact effectively with their infants. In practice, in many of the interventions both aspects are provided and their independent effects are hard to distinguish. What differs are the outcomes that have been measured. Whatever the focus, the mother is valued and evaluated by the extent to which she produces and nurtures children who make 'the grade'.

The background to the design of these interventions reflects the findings of earlier studies suggesting that the way in which the traditional maternal and child health services are organized and delivered, was a factor for many mothers who did not attend clinics or take up classes in parenting. Services were often experienced as particularly problematic and stressful by working-class mothers (McIntosh, 1992). A common theme in the research (e.g. Mayall and Foster, 1989) is the lack of client-centred services, with long waiting times, lack of childcare, and difficulties relating to transport and cost, all cited as barriers to attending. The services did not provide anything which was fundamentally helpful from the perspective of those at risk. Professionals were not adequately trained in the manner and sensitivity with which they delivered advice and information, and this could act to create barriers between themselves and those they sought to help. Health visitors, for example, are an almost universal service and a potentially important source of support and information for mothers. However, evaluations of the role of health visitors have found that when advice is given which is contrary to the belief system of the mother, she may simply stop seeing the health visitor (McIntosh, 1986). Advice on weaning and the positioning of the baby during sleep are examples where well-intentioned advice has had limited influence on the most deprived families. This underlines the importance of the perceived appropriateness of a service and the link with take-up. As Pugh says, 'It is often easier for professionals to provide services that they think parents and children ought to have, than to take time to talk to and listen to parents' (Pugh, 1996: 26).

## (II) PROVIDING OR ENHANCING SOCIAL SUPPORT

Epidemiological research on depression has documented the close association between the mother's mental state and the amount of contact with kin and friendship networks. The place of social support within causal models differs according to whether it is seen as a cause or an effect of the mother's behaviour (Parks, Lenz and Jenkins, 1992). Crnic and Stormshak (1997) say, 'it is critical to note that support may serve as a main effect on parental well-being, as well as a buffer during stressful conditions'. Social support may be seen as naturally occurring as part of the mother's network, or as something that can be artificially provided. It is not obvious how much the latter can substitute for the former. The providers of social support have included highly trained professionals such as midwives, as well as health visitors, volunteers and volunteer mothers.

The Social Support and Pregnancy Outcome study (SSPO) (Oakley, Rajan and Grant, 1990; Oakley, 1992) (see Appendix) is a British example of a randomized control trial which has used an intervention delivered by trained midwives to provide social support. In the obstetrically 'high risk' group involved in the research, the working-class mothers had less naturally occurring social support from family and friends, and the father of the baby was more likely to be a source of stress than a support (Oakley and Rajan, 1991). This intervention worked well in the short term both for mothers and babies. What the mothers valued most was that the supporter had 'listened', although working-class mothers were more likely to value the advice element of the midwife's package of support. It may be that the combination of expert and expertise was valued.

In contrast, the Community Mothers Programme (Johnson, Howell and Molloy, 1993; Johnson and Molloy, 1995) (see Appendix) provided support from volunteers who were experienced mothers and who lived in the same community as the 'at risk' mothers. Projects such as this, which are based upon the 'buddying' principle, reduce the distance created by professionals' claims of expertise. Parents who need this kind of support are also less likely to be intimidated by the sanctions which professionals are empowered to use. Supervision for the volunteer mothers was provided by a trained nurse, and although the intervention was concerned with promoting 'right parenting' (health care, nutrition and child development) it is probable that an element of social support was provided. At the end of the study, mothers living in very deprived circumstances were less likely to report being tired, feeling miserable, or staying indoors. As with the multi-agency centres, anecdotal accounts of this and other interventions involving volunteers, suggest that committed, energetic and charismatic individuals are an important feature of the success of programmes such as this.

## (III) MATERNAL HEALTH

A Scottish intervention, in which health visitors provided counselling after a short focused course, claimed success in treating postnatal depression with home visits (Holden, Sagovsky and Cox, 1989). It was recognized that taking the service to the target group was an important element of this intervention, as it avoided the difficulty that many mothers of young children have in getting to community facilities. These difficulties may be of physical access, such as using public transport, getting prams up and down stairs etc., or they may be those of motivation or mental state.

Many studies have documented the high prevalence of postnatal depression and depression in general, among working-class mothers of young children (Brown and Harris, 1978), with a very high proportion experiencing clinical depression. One study (McIntosh, 1993) found up to 60 per cent of predominantly married women in a working-class sample with significant symptoms. The SSPO (Oakley, 1992) found that housing tenure (living in rented property) was the best predictor of the mothers' psychological outcomes.

NEWPIN (see Appendix) has provided support (social

involvement, therapy and training) for mothers in very difficult circumstances and has claimed some success. Those mothers who used the service valued the opportunities for being and talking with other mothers in the same situation. An evaluation of the service (Oakley *et al.*, 1995) found that less than half of the referrals had made use of the service, and of those who had used it, only half had found it helpful. Those who did not use the service felt that either it did not meet what they perceived as their needs, or they had problems getting to the centre. At first glance, this volunteer service has replicated many of the problems found in traditional health centres.

There have been many interventions which have targeted particular health behaviours in pregnant mothers or mothers of young children. Attempts at smoking cessation or reduction of smoking in these groups have generally not been very effective. Graham (1994) interviewed mothers who smoked, who reported that their continuing 'risk taking' behaviour was the result of their need to provide themselves with some means of relaxation and enjoyment in situations of high stress. Failure to take account of the integrated nature of this behaviour, but at the same time providing mothers with information about the dangers of smoking probably acts only to increase anxiety and stress.

## (IV) INTERVENING TO ENHANCE THE TASK OF MOTHERING INFANTS AND CHILDREN

There is evidence that providing advice and information, especially when the content and timing are controlled by the mother, promotes rather than diminishes self-esteem. Advice to mothers during pregnancy or the early years may be about feeding, nutrition, hygiene, providing appropriate stimulation and dealing with developmental problems. Most interventions in this area have, in effect, confounded the effects of social support with those of information provision, so that it is difficult to know whether it is the informational or emotional aspects that have had positive effects on mothering behaviour.

The Community Mothers' Programme, discussed earlier, was a study of first-time mothers which focused on encouraging mothers to interact in a 'constructive' way with their infants. The intervention group was reported by the assessing nurse to be more likely to have received all of their primary immunisations, to be read to daily, played more cognitive games and were exposed to more nursery rhymes.

A recent review (Blair and Ramey, 1997) of the literature on interventions with babies at risk as a result of low birth weight, argued that the most effective interventions took place when the baby was very young. The authors characterized the huge literature on this topic according to the duration and intensity of the interventions, and the extent to which it was parent- or child-focused. It was concluded that interventions with parents in the child's home were more effective than those which delivered the intervention to the child. Working with mothers was more effective, and this justified 'a continued focus on parents and an emphasis on the improvement of educational and interactional routines at home'.

## c) Intervening in parenting

There has been a strong focus in recent years upon interventions designed to improve parenting skills. This is consistent with research evidence that family functioning, rather than family structure, has the greatest impact upon outcomes for children (McFarlane, Bellissimo and Norman, 1995; Utting, 1995).

### (I) PARENT EDUCATION

Parenting courses are offered in a variety of contexts and by a range of different organizations. Some, such as Home-Start, provide courses in parenting skills as part of a general package of support offered to parents of young children. Parents often make the initial contact with the organization, but it also receives referrals from health visitors, general practitioners, social workers and other professionals involved with families with young children. Home-Start provides trained volunteers who make home visits, provide practical help, advice and support as requested. Home-Start is a national consultancy organization and its service operates within a peer support rather than an hierarchical model, and with the aim of building up parents' self-confidence so that they can then benefit from local services and networks of support (Frost et al., 1996).

Within a broad spectrum of parenting education, some programmes, such as that led by Patterson in Oregon (Patterson, Chamberlain and Reid, 1982) specifically target parents with skill deficits when dealing with their child's anti-social behaviour, which is often accompanied by hyperactivity and early offending. In addition to the standard behavioural recipe of setting firm boundaries, establishing a clear system of rewards and punishments, Patterson's intervention also supports parents in preventing conflicts from getting out of control.

Patterson's research, although promising, has some important limitations. A relatively high proportion of parents drop out of the programmes (20 per cent), and an even higher proportion (one-third) refused to participate in a follow-up evaluation after one year (Communities that Care, 1996). The reasons for both the high level of attrition and the reported improvements in boys' behaviour in those who continued to participate have not been fully explained.

New research in progress (Scott and Sylva, 1999) is seeking to compare different outcomes for parents of five-year-old children with behavioural problems. One group have been assigned to a programme of parent education in which they learn to manage problem behaviour, and are also encouraged to be actively involved in helping their child to read. A second group of parents (also of children with behavioural problems) is receiving standard services. Parents and children without behaviour problems form a third group. The findings from this research should assist in the development of more effective interventions for this particular group of children and their parents.

Difficulties in evaluating parenting programmes (many combine self-reports, observed changes in parental and child behaviour in day care centres, and social services case notes) influence the extent to which claims can be made about their effectiveness. Some evaluations have adopted a before-and-after approach but have not included control groups (Utting, 1996). Barlow (1997) reviewed 255 studies of group-based parenting education and found only 18 that were of a sufficiently high standard to enable an evaluation of effectiveness.

Questions have also been raised about the appropriateness of parenting training for families that are dealing with multiple sources of stress such as poverty, social isolation or maternal depression. In general, the research suggests that parenting courses are a useful tool within a broad range of potential supports to families, particularly where an accurate assessment has been made by the parents themselves, or others, of the need for information and skills training (Miller and Prinz, 1990). However, if parenting courses are used as a stand-alone intervention in inappropriate circumstances, they are unlikely to have any lasting benefits. Families with long-standing and complex problems are likely to require a complex package of long-term support.

## (II) FAMILY CENTRES

Family centres (social services and voluntary sector based) also focus on family relationships, but it is unclear how central the child is in this process. It appears that family support services are effective for children to the extent that they are able to relieve family stress (Gibbons, Thorpe and Wilkinson, 1990). Gibbons and colleagues conducted a comparison between two different models of social service delivery: one a centralized service organized along traditional lines, and the other a decentralized service. In the latter case, social workers de-camped to a community building which was shared with other services and voluntary sector groups. Users of the new-style family centre reported greater ease in gaining access to day care and social work support. They also felt that the centre strengthened their local support base which included family members, friends and neighbours.

Similar benefits for families have been associated with open access family centres, many of which are run by voluntary sector organizations. Open access centres can also offer non-stigmatizing services which have the potential to be responsive to users.

## (III) FAMILY MEDIATION

Family Mediation is another style of intervention in family conflict which could have potential benefits for children. The Family Mediation Project helps parents to resolve conflicts over a range of issues, such as child custody and access, housing, and maintenance payments. A comparison has been made between the effectiveness in reducing levels of parental conflict of 'child-focused negotiations' which cover questions of child custody and access only, and 'all issues' negotiations which cover all causes of conflict during divorce proceedings. McCarthy and Walker (1996) found that couples using the 'all issues' negotiations experienced a reduced level of conflict compared with couples who participated in the child-focused mediation. The former group also incurred lower legal costs than their counterparts in the child-focused mediation. It is notable that despite the 'child-focused' terminology, children do not participate in these discussions.

## d) Intervening in the community

There have been few evaluations of broad-based interventions at community level in the UK since the Education Priority Area Projects were established in the 1960s. The outcomes from these evaluations are unclear. It has been argued that targeting a geographical area is not necessarily an efficient way of targeting children from deprived backgrounds, since most areas contain a social mix of families. There are also issues of the impact of relative versus absolute deprivation. Children living in rural areas were also often excluded by an area targeted approach.

The Atlanta Project in the US provides one example of a promising approach at the community level. The project was established in 1995 and has not yet been evaluated. It may, however, provide a useful model for a geographically targeted approach to reducing the negative effects of poverty on children's lives. The project covers large sections of Atlanta and the surrounding counties with the highest levels of deprivation. Given the difficulties in targeting such a large area, subdivisions or 'clusters' have been set up, each with their own co-ordinator. These 'clusters' are supported by a central office who 'loan' out experts or secondees in various fields, such as education, health, public safety, economic development, child welfare and development. A university is also partnered with each cluster. Each cluster has a plan and a number of task forces working around locally identified problems.

The guiding principles behind the Atlanta Project are that children and young people are part of a wider community and their needs should be integrated into a strategy for community regeneration. The project also operates according to an ethos of 'community empowerment' and actively involves community representatives in a multi-agency partnership. The project also takes the view that attempting to change the outcomes for children in deprived areas requires long term investment.

It should be noted that community development approaches of this kind require concentrated effort at the 'grass roots' level, as well as between different agencies, and may require a lead-in period before beneficial outcomes for children can be identified.

## e) The national context

At the national level, governments have the power to shape public policy in relation to services for children. They can also frame legislation which would enable families to help themselves through a more equitable approach to taxation and benefits. For example, an increase in benefit for pregnant women has been shown to be effective in reducing the number of premature and low birth weight babies (which are risk factors for later ill-health and under-achievement). Research has shown that mothers are more likely than fathers to prioritize food for their children over other needs. A mechanism which increases the material resources of pregnant women can significantly reduce the risk factors for parental stress and child development which lead to poor outcomes.

In the past, services to children have developed in a fragmented way. This is partly the result of the differing responsibilities of government departments, but also to a certain extent because children have been viewed as the private responsibility of the family. However, if children are perceived as a societal responsibility, the scope for improving their life chances becomes far wider. Without a national context which is supportive of families, 'interventions' run the danger of continuing this pattern of fragmentation and of only dealing with the symptoms, rather than the causes of social exclusion.

# 5
# Conclusions

Conclusions about the effectiveness of early interventions fall into two broad categories. The first category relates to general principles which should guide the development of all interventions during the early years. A second and related category focuses on the issues raised by specific categories of intervention, such as pre-school education or social support for mothers.

It should be noted, however, that the conclusions we have drawn are based upon published studies and that those interventions which have been effective or have shown promise are more likely to be written about than those which have failed. In short, and despite the relatively small number of evaluations that have been conducted, our conclusions are likely to be subject to a publication bias.

## GENERAL PRINCIPLES OF INTERVENTION

At the level of implementation, why do some projects work and others not? In terms of general principles of intervention, our conclusions are grouped under the following headings:
- community participation
- local interventions
- matching needs with interventions.

### *Community participation*

There has, in general, been rather little emphasis in evaluation on investigating the mechanisms by which an intervention is effective, or fails to be so. Community support or participation appears to be a part of many successful interventions, although not all, and it is not always identified as a contributory factor. It seems probable, rather than proven, that community participation is an important contributory factor in successful interventions, for a number of reasons. The mechanisms of action have to be inferred, but it is likely that community participation works at many levels, including the reduction of any stigma associated in participating in an intervention, and in enhancing self-esteem, and as source of social support to individuals in that community.

*Projects are more likely to be successful if they promote the involvement of local people in their planning and implementation.*
Projects initiated by statutory services also appear to be more successful if they listen to, and involve local people. Community involvement has two main effects: interventions, whether led by the voluntary or statutory sector, are able to draw upon and stimulate the shared concern of local people for each other and for their environment. Second, local people (parents and children) become active participants, rather than passive recipients of services.

The promotion of community participation does not mean that all interventions should be run by voluntary groups or that statutory services should shift the responsibility for offering help onto community groups. The main point here is that interventions which actively involve local people can provide a solid basis upon which to build a spectrum of family support services. Community projects may not be able to provide the professional support which some families need, but they can perform a valuable role in referring families on to other forms of support.

## Local interventions

There are various advantages and disadvantages to targeting, and no empirical evidence that compares targeted interventions with those that are not specifically targeted, but in general it appears that the benefits of targeted interventions, if carried out well, outweigh the disadvantages. Essentially:

*Community participation can be greatly facilitated by interventions which target specific areas.*
Localized interventions also have a number of other advantages. They are more likely to:

- improve access to local services and support
- show sensitivity to the social and cultural diversity of local communities
- facilitate partnership working
- draw upon the energy of charismatic individuals.

*Targeting interventions at a specific area reduces the geographical distance between families and services,* and this has shown to be an important way of improving access to services by reducing waiting times, transport costs and other difficulties.

*Localized interventions also have the potential for reducing the social distance between service provider and user.* The evidence strongly suggests that interventions are more likely to be effective if they are provided by people of a similar social background or are provided by professionals with sufficient empathy to cross the professional/lay divide.

*Professionals should receive training so that they become aware of the professional norms which create barriers between themselves and the people they help.* The research evidence indicates that the manner in which advice or help is given is important. If information or advice is given in an insensitive way, at an inappropriate time, or is contrary to the belief system of the recipient, it is not likely to be effective, and may result in the individual ceasing to use a service. A service will not be effective if it is not taken up or used by local people.

*Interventions targeted at a geographical area can help to make working in partnership more effective.* One of the key themes in this regard is the importance of partnership across different agencies and between local people and service providers. With a partnership model, opportunities for responding to families and communities in an holistic way are maximized. It must also be acknowledged, however, that while the principle of partnership working is desirable, it may be hard to achieve in practice. Partnership working tends to be time-consuming and may operate only at the level of information-sharing, rather than in a genuinely strategic way. A designated budget and the appointment of an officer with a co-ordination role may help to limit the divisions which can occur between different 'stakeholders' within a partnership.

*An intangible, but important explanation for why some interventions work relates to the charisma effect.* Outside of scientifically designed and evaluated interventions, promising local community projects are often led by charismatic figures who have the energy and enthusiasm to attract the co-operation of other local people. They are also successful in promoting their work to funders and thereby attract resources to areas of need.

## Matching needs with interventions

The principle that interventions should match needs operates at a number of levels:

- the needs of individual families
- the needs of families according to different stages (e.g. pregnancy, early parenthood) and in relation to differences in resources between families.

*The research strongly supports the principle that, in order to be effective, interventions should closely match the needs of individual families.* Some parents and children may require low-level support to get them through a difficult patch; other families may need a range of support, including professional help, over a long period. We have seen, for example, that parenting courses may be of benefit to some parents and not to others. A sensitive process of assessment is required so that an intervention can be selected which has the best chance of meeting the needs of an individual family. This general principle presupposes the availability of a number of possible options and underlines the need for multi-level *and* localized forms of intervention.

*A single intervention is unlikely to produce positive outcomes for parents or children over the long term.* A single 'inoculation' targeting a specific aspect of the child's or parent's social world is of limited benefit if it ignores wider familial and social contexts. In this report, we have discussed a range of interventions according to various tiers: the child, the mother, parents, the neighbourhood, and the national context. Examples of successful and promising interventions suggest that more than one of these levels has to be targeted at the same time. The 'recipe' should reflect the needs of the local community but the ingredients might include, for example, support for the mother after pregnancy together with quality pre-school for children, and the development of play facilities. Each intervention then has the chance of creating a momentum for positive change.

*Resources should be targeted at varieties of need in terms of levels of intensity and at various times in the family life cycle.* Some families, because of their higher levels of need, will draw upon different interventions, and therefore absorb more resources than families with short-term or low-level needs. The availability of this range of options reduces the risk of stigmatization, provides a preventive element and reduces the resentment caused by the targeting of resources solely at those most in need.

*Initiatives which are targeted geographically carry the risk of stigmatizing communities but also provide a useful mechanism for reducing poverty in areas with high levels of deprivation.* We have argued that interventions work best if they are localized and this implies a need to target resources geographically. The possible consequences of this approach are that communities acquire stigmatizing labels. On the other hand, some have argued that targeting resources at those most in need, and therefore most at risk of social exclusion, represents both a social and fiscal imperative. A balance needs to be struck between these two positions. Geographically targeted interventions should be presented in a positive light as mechanisms for reducing inequality rather than in a 'problem-centred' way. These initiatives could also be complemented and reinforced by family-friendly tax and benefits systems which support all families.

*An ethos of community participation together with the availability of a range of interventions can operate as protective factors.* The availability of safe and stimulating play spaces, for example, represents a low-level intervention which is both non-stigmatizing and supportive of the physical and social development of all children. At the other end of the spectrum, a more resource-intensive intervention, such as pre-school education, can be differentially applied in terms of how resources are utilized within a given area. This might not necessarily mean that better off families would be excluded, but rather that they might be invited to pay towards the cost of such a service and thereby subsidize services for poorer families. The development of quality services designed to counteract the effects of social inequality can help to protect against stigma, and support the more intangible factor of confidence and self-esteem at the community level.

## WHAT WORKS? SPECIFIC CATEGORIES OF INTERVENTIONS

In addition to the general principles of intervention outlined above, there are a number of specific kinds of intervention which have shown particular success.

## *Pre-school education*

*The evidence strongly suggests that quality pre-school education is effective because it increases the child's receptivity for learning.* This is of crucial importance for children from deprived backgrounds who may have few resources at home to support their early learning. The first years of primary school can be a struggle for these children as they try to catch up with children who have a more stimulating home environment or parents with a greater awareness of the educative value of play.

*Some of the most effective pre-school early interventions involve parents in their child's cognitive development.* This can occur at home or in a pre-school centre. The value of such an approach is that it encourages parents to take an interest in their child's education, which has been shown to be a key factor influencing their educational attainment. Involving parents can also be of benefit to parents themselves who may have had poor experiences at school and who may relate to the school environment with fear or negativity. We could conclude that pre-school projects which involve parents are successful because they increase a sense of mastery and therefore self-esteem of both parents and children.

*However, parental involvement in the child's education may not be so important for older children.* Reading Recovery, for example, was shown to be successful in older children possibly because a minimal level of parental participation was required. In some cases, therefore, parental participation may not be appropriate and we should guard against it becoming a rigid expectation.

*The most effective projects appear to utilize children's instinct for play and fun and to allow them scope to be physically active.* Play has an important developmental role during the early years. Enjoyment and fun are important both in terms of the efficacy of the intervention and in terms of increasing the likelihood of take-up. Conversely, ineffective pre-school interventions are more likely to make early learning a burden for the child. Through an over-emphasis upon the importance of education, interventions run the risk of hurrying children through their early years in order to get them to the more important business of primary school education. One of the qualities which many adults appreciate in children is their ability to be 'in the moment'. We should be wary of depriving children of opportunities for enjoyment in the present.

*Self-esteem is important in securing positive long-term outcomes for parents and children.* For children, a problem-solving curriculum, in which a relationship of dialogue with the adult is fostered, appears to increase the child's sense of achievement and confidence and reduce shame. For adults, parenting classes and the availability of other forms of social support appear to increase parents' self-confidence. A central theme here is the quality of relationship, whether between a parent and child, a professional and a parent, or a professional and a child. Supportive interest and concern, not overlaid by authoritarian strictures, appear to work well with both adults and children in that they help to strengthen inner resilience and self-esteem.

## Community support for parents

Currently, mothers continue to be the main carers of children, and interventions targeted at the mother are generally effective, at least in the short term, if they are responsive to the mother's expressed needs and are flexible. 'Community mothers' and other social support interventions for mothers with young children provide an example of this kind of intervention. Feeling supported in the neighbourhood can reduce feelings of social isolation in mothers, and protect against depression.

*The mother's mental health is a key factor influencing the general level of resilience within the family to internal and external pressures.* The mother's resilience may also have an important influence on the long-term outcomes for children. Interventions which reduce the stress upon mothers therefore benefit children indirectly. These interventions may target an increase in support networks *outside* the family or may increase support *within* the family by, for example, involving fathers more in care tasks. However, few interventions involve fathers. Approaches which encourage the father and other family members to share in care tasks have been shown to reduce mothers' stress levels. This is an aspect of family support which future interventions could pay more attention to.

## THE NATIONAL CONTEXT

*Some interventions at the national level have considerable scope for intervening in the lives of poor families regardless of where they live.* Mention has already been made of family-friendly tax and benefits systems.

## *Principles for future implementation*

The research shows that, while every effort should be made to formulate interventions on available information on 'what works', the imposition of rigid blueprints should be avoided and is contrary to the desirability of a 'bottom up' rather than 'top down' approach. Interventions that are successful appear to be flexible to local needs, and interactive and responsive, in taking account of the feelings and needs of participants. We would therefore suggest that the principles outlined above should provide a general direction for interventions which may be developed at the local level, according to local needs.

# REFERENCES

Alderson, P. with Highfield School (1996), *Changing our school.* London: Institute of Education, University of London.

Alderson, P., Brill, S., Chalmers, I., Fuller, R., Hinkley-Smith, P., MacDonald, G., Newman,T., Oakley, A., Roberts, H. and Ward, H. (1996), *What works: effective social interventions in child welfare.* London: Social Science Research Unit, Institute of Education, and Barnardos.

Amato, P. and Keith, B. (1991), 'Parental divorce and the well-being of children: a meta analysis'. *Psychological Bulletin,* 110, 26–46.

Bailey, D. (1997), 'Evaluating the effectiveness of curriculum alternatives for infants and preschoolers at high risk'. In M. Guralnick (ed.), *The effectiveness of early intervention.* Baltimore: Brookes.

Barlow, J. (1997), *Systematic review of the effectiveness of parent-training programmes in improving behaviour problems in children aged 3–19 yrs.* Health Services Research Unit Report, Health Services Research Unit, Department of Public Health, University of Oxford.

Barnett, W. and Escobar, C. (1990), 'Economic costs and benefits of early intervention'. In S. Meisels and J. Shonkoff (eds), *Handbook of early childhood intervention.* Cambridge: Cambridge University Press.

Belsky, J. and Vondra, J. (1989), 'Lessons from child abuse: the determinants of parenting'. In D. Cicchetti and V. Carlson (eds), *Child maltreatment. Theory and research on the causes and consequences of child abuse and neglect.* Cambridge: Cambridge University Press.

Berrueta-Clement, J., Schweinhart, L., Barnett, W., Epstein, A. and Weikart, D. (1984), *Changed lives: the effects of the Perry Preschool Programme on youth through age 19.* Michigan: High/Scope Press.

Blair, C. and Ramey, C. (1997), 'Early intervention for low-birth-weight infants and the path to second-generation research'. In M. Guralnick (ed.), *The effectiveness of early intervention.* Baltimore: Brookes.

Blaxter, M. (1986), 'Longitudinal studies in Britain'. In R. Wilkinson (ed.), *Class and health*. London: Tavistock.

Brannen, J. and O'Brien, M. (1996), *Children in families: Research and Policy*. London: Falmer Press.

Brannen, J., Moss, P., Owen, C. and Wale, C. (1997), *Mothers, fathers and employment. Parents and the labour market in Britain, 1984–1994*. London: DfEE/ Institute of Education, University of London.

Brown, G. and Harris, T. (1978), *Social origins of depression*. London: Tavistock.

Bruner, J. (1983), *Child's talk: learning to use language*. Oxford: Oxford University Press.

Buttigieg, M. (1995), 'Difficult issues of evaluation'. *Health Visitor*, 68, 225.

Bynner, J. (1998), '*Which children are most at risk of becoming socially excluded?*' In Comprehensive Spending Review: cross departmental review of provision for young children: supporting papers, volume 1. London: H.M. Treasury, July 1998.

Bynner, J. and Steedman, J. (1995), *Difficulties with basic skills*. London: Basic Skills Agency.

Clay, M.M. (1979), *The early detection of reading difficulties: a diagnostic survey with recovery procedures*. London: Heinemann Educational.

Clay, M. (1991), *Becoming literate: the construction of inner control*. Auckland: Heinemann.

Communities that Care (1996), *Communities that Care prevention strategies: a research guide to what works*. Seattle: Developmental Research and Programmes, Inc.

Conroy, S. and Smith, M. (1999), *Exploring infant health*. London: Foundation for the Study of Infant Deaths.

Cox, A., Pound, A., Mills, M., Puckering, C. and Owen, A. (1991), 'Evaluation of a home visiting and befriending scheme for young mothers: Newpin'. *Journal of the Royal Society of Medicine*, 84, 217–220.

Cox, A. D. (1993), 'Befriending young mothers'. *British Journal of Psychiatry*, 163, 618.

Crnic, K. and Stormshak, E. (1997), 'The effectiveness of providing social support for families of children at risk'. In M. Guralnick (ed.), *The effectiveness of early intervention*. Baltimore: Brookes.

David, T. (1994), 'Making a difference for children "in need". Educare services'. In T. David (ed.) *Working together for young children, multi-professionalism in action*. London: Routledge.

— (1996), 'Curriculum in the early years'. In G. Pugh (ed.), *Contemporary issues in the early years. Working collaboratively for children*. London: National Children's Bureau.

Drake, B. and Pandey, S. (1996), 'Understanding the relationship between neighborhood poverty and specific types of child maltreatment'. *Child Abuse and Neglect*, 20, 1003–1018.

Ermisch, J. and Francesconi, M. (1997), *Family Matters*. Working papers of the ESRC Research Centre on Micro-Social Change (Paper 97-1). Colchester: University of Essex.

European Childcare Network (1992), *Quality of Services for Young Children*. Brussels: European Commission.

Farran, D. (1990), 'Effects of intervention with disadvantaged and disabled children: a decade review'. In S. Meisels and J. Shonkoff (eds), *Handbook of early childhood intervention*. Cambridge: Cambridge University Press.

Farrington, D. (1995), 'The development of offending and antisocial behaviour from childhood: key findings from the Cambridge study in delinquent development'. *Journal of Child Psychology and Psychiatry*, 36, 929–964.

Frost, N., Johnson, L., Stein, M. and Wallis, L. (1996), *Negotiated friendship: Home-Start and the delivery of family support*. Leicester: Home-Start UK.

Gibbons, J., Thorpe, S. and Wilkinson, P. (1990), *Family support and prevention: studies in local areas*. London: HMSO.

Graham, H. (1994), 'Gender and class as dimensions of smoking behaviour in Britain: insights from a survey of mothers'. *Social Science and Medicine*, 38, 691–698.

Gregg, P. and Machin, S. (1998), 'Child development and success or failure in the youth labour market'. *Discussion Papers, number 397*. London: Centre for Economic Performance.

Guralnick, M. (ed.) (1997), *The effectiveness of early intervention*. Baltimore: Brookes.

Guralnick, M. (1997), 'Second-generation research in the field of early intervention'. In M. Guralnick (ed.), *The effectiveness of early intervention*. Baltimore: Brookes.

Halpern, R. (1990), 'Community-based early intervention'. In S. Meisels and J. Shonkoff (eds), *Handbook of early childhood intervention*. Cambridge: Cambridge University Press.

Hawkins, J. D., Catalano, R.F., Morrison, D.M., O'Donnell, J., Abbott, R. D. and Day, L.E. (1992), 'The Seattle Development Project: effects of the first four years on protective factors and problem behaviors'. In J. McCord and R. Tremblay (eds), *The prevention of antisocial behavior*. New York: Guilford.

Hohmann, M., Barnet, B. and Weikart, D. (1979), *Young children in action: a manual for pre-school educators*. Ypsilanti: High/Scope Educational Research Foundation.

Holden, J., Sagovsky, R. and Cox, J. (1989), 'Counselling in a general practice setting: controlled study of health visitor intervention in treatment of postnatal depression'. *British Medical Journal*, 298, 223–6.

Holtermann, S. (1995), *Investing in young children: a reassessment of the cost of an education and day care service*. London: National Children's Bureau.

—— (1998), *Weighing it up: applying economic evaluations to social welfare programmes*. York: Joseph Rowntree Foundation.

Hurry, J. and Sylva, K. (1997), *The long term effects of two interventions for children with reading difficulties*. London: QCA.

Jackson, S. (1994), 'Young children in the care system'. In T. David (ed.), *Working together for young children, multi-professionalism in action.* London: Routledge.

Johnson, Z. and Molloy, B. (1995), 'The community mothers programme – empowerment of parents by parents'. *Children and Society*, 9, 73–85.

Johnson, Z., Howell, F. and Molloy, B. (1993), 'Community mothers programme: randomised controlled trial of a non-professional intervention in parenting'. *British Medical Journal*, 306, 1449–1452.

Jowett, S. and Sylva, K. (1986), 'Does kind of Pre-School Matter?' *Educational Research*, 28, 21–31.

Kiernan, K., Land, H. and Lewis, J. (1998), *Lone motherhood in the twentieth century.* Oxford: Oxford University Press.

Kuh, D. and Wadsworth, M. (1993), 'Physical health status at 36 years in a British national birth cohort.' *Social Science and Medicine*, 37, 905–916.

Kumar, V. (1993), *Poverty and inequality in the UK: The effects on children.* London: National Children's Bureau.

Lazar, I. and Darlington, R. (1982*), Lasting effects of early education: a report from the Consortium for Longitudinal Studies.* Monographs of the Society for Research in Child Development, (number 195), 47, 1–151.

Lee, B., Brooks-Gunn, J. and Schnur, E. (1988), 'Does Head Start work? A one-year follow-up comparison of disadvantaged children attending Head-Start, no pre-school and other pre-school programmes'. *Developmental Psychology*, 24, 210–222.

Logan, S. and Spencer, N. (1996), 'Smoking and other health related behaviour in the social and environmental context'. *Archives of Disease in Childhood*, 74, 176–179.

McCarthy, P. and Walker, J. (1996), *Evaluating the longer term impact of family mediation.* Newcastle upon Tyne: Relate Centre for Family Studies.

MacDonald, G. and Roberts, H. (1995), *What Works in the Early Years?* Ilford: Barnardos.

McFarlane, A., Bellissimo, A. and Norman, G. (1995), 'Family structure, family functioning and adolescent well-being: the transcendent influence of parental style'. *Journal of Child Psychology and Psychiatry*, 36, 847–864.

McGee, R., Share, D., Moffitt, T., Williams, S. and Silva, P. (1988), 'Reading disability, behaviour problems and juvenile delinquency'. In D. Saklofske and S. Eysenck (eds), *Individual differences in children and adolescents: international perspectives*. London: Hodder and Stoughton.

McGuire, J. and Richman, N. (1986), 'The prevalence of behaviour problems in three types of preschool group.' *Journal of Child Psychology and Psychiatry*, 27, 455–472.

McGurk, H., Caplan, M., Hennessy, E. and Moss, P. (1993), 'Controversy, theory and social context in contemporary day care research'. *Journal of Child Psychology and Psychiatry*, 34, 3–23.

McIntosh, J. (1986), 'Weaning practices in a sample of working class primiparae'. *Child: Care, Health and Development*, 12, 215–226.

— (1992), 'The perception and use of child health clinics in a sample of working class families'. *Child: Care, Health and Development*, 18, 133–150.

— (1993), 'Postpartum depression: women's help-seeking behaviour and perceptions of cause'. *Journal of Advanced Nursing*, 18, 178–184.

McKey, H. R., Condellli, L., Ganson, H., Barrett, B., McConkey, C. and Plantz, M. (1985), *The impact of Head Start on children, families and communities. Final report of the Head Start evaluation, synthesis and utilisation project*. The Head Start Bureau. Administration for Children Youth and Families. Washington DC: Office of Human Development Services, US Department of Health and Human Services.

Makins, V. (1997), *Not just a Nursery ... Multi-agency early years centres in action*. London: National Children's Bureau.

Maughan, B., Gray, G. and Rutter, M. (1985), 'Reading retardation and antisocial behaviour: a follow-up into employment'. *Journal of Child Psychology and Psychiatry*, 26, 741–758.

Maughan, B., Pickles, A., Hagell, A., Rutter, M. and Yule, W. (1996), 'Reading problems and antisocial behaviour: developmental trends and comorbidity'. *Journal of Child Psychology and Psychiatry*, 37, 405–417.

Mayall, B. and Foster, M. (1989), *Child health care: living with children, working for children*. Oxford: Heinemann.

Melhuish, E. and Moss, P. (1991), *Daycare for young children*. London: Routledge.

Meisels, S. and Shonkoff, K, (1990), *Handbook of early childhood intervention*. Cambridge: Cambridge University Press.

Miller, G. and Prinz, R. (1990), 'Enhancement of social learning family interventions for childhood conduct disorders'. *Psychological Bulletin*, 108, 291–307.

Mooney, A. and Munton, A. (1997), *Research and policy in early childhood services: time for a new agenda*. London: Thomas Coram Research Unit.

Oakley, A. (1992), *Social support and motherhood: natural history of a research project*. Oxford: Basil Blackwood.

— (1992), 'Social support in pregnancy: methodology and findings of a 1 year follow-up study'. *Journal of Reproductive and Infant Psychology*, 10, 219–231.

— (1996), 'Who's afraid of the randomised controlled trial?: the challenge of evaluating the potential of social interventions'. In P. Alderson *et al. What works: effective social interventions in child welfare*. London: SSRU, Institute of Education, and Barnardos.

Oakley, A. and Rajan, L. (1991), 'Social class and social support: the same or different?' *Sociology*, 25, 31–59.

Oakley, A., Rajan, L. and Grant, A. (1990), 'Social support and pregnancy outcome'. *British Journal of Obstetrics and Gynaecology*, 97, 155–162.

Oakley, A., Mauthner, M., Rajan, L. and Turner, H. (1995), 'Supporting vulnerable families: an evaluation of NEWPIN'. *Health Visitor*, 68, 188–191.

Osborn, A. F. and Millbank, J. E. (1987), *The effects of early education: a report from the child health and education study*. Oxford: Oxford University Press.

OPCS (1994), *Population Trends 77*, London: HMSO.

Parks, P., Lenz, E. and Jenkins, L. (1992), 'The role of social support and stressors for mothers and infants'. *Child: Care, Health and Development*, 18, 151–171.

Patterson, G.R., Chamberlain, P. and Reid, J.B. (1982), 'A comparative evaluation of a parent training programme'. *Behaviour Therapy*, 13, 638–650.

Petrie, P. (1994), *Play and Care*. London: HMSO.

Pound, A. (1994), *NEWPIN: a befriending and therapeutic network for carers of young children*. London: HMSO/National NEWPIN.

Power, S., Whitty, G. and Youdell, D. (1995), *No place to learn: homelessness and education*. London: Shelter.

Puckering, C., Rogers, J., Mills, M., Cox, A. D. and Mattson-Graff, M. (1994), 'Process and evaluation of a group intervention for mothers with parenting difficulties'. *Child Abuse Review*, 3, 299–310.

Pugh, G. (1996), A policy for early childhood services? In G. Pugh (ed.), *Contemporary issues in the early years. Working collaboratively for children*. London: National Children's Bureau.

— (1998), *Children at risk of becoming socially excluded: an introduction to the 'problem'*. In Comprehensive Spending Review: cross departmental review of provision for young children: supporting papers, volume 1. London: H.M. Treasury, July 1998.

Pugh, G., De'Ath, E. and Smith, C. (1994), *Confident parents, confident children. Policy and practice in parent education and support*. London: National Children's Bureau.

Robinson, P. (1997), *Literacy, numeracy and economic performance*. London: Centre for Economic Performance.

Robertson, D. and Symons, J. (1996), *Do peer groups matter? Peer group versus schooling effects on academic attainment*. Discussion Paper No. 311. London: Centre for Economic Performance.

Rutter, M. (1974), 'Dimensions of parenthood: some myths and some suggestions'. In *The Family in Society: dimensions of parenthood*. Department of Health and Social Security, London: HMSO.

— (1995), *Psychosocial disturbances in young people: challenges for prevention*. Cambridge: Cambridge University Press.

Rutter, M., Maughan, B., Mortimore, P. and Ouston, J. (1979), *Fifteen thousand hours: secondary schools and their effects on children*. London: Open Books.

Schweinhart, L.J. and Weikart, D. P. (1980), *Young children grow up: the effects of the Perry pre-school program on youths through age 15*. Monographs of the High/Scope Educational Research Foundation, No 7. Ypsilanti: High/Scope Educational Foundation.

Schweinhart, L., Barnes, H. and Weikart, D. (1993), *A summary of significant benefits: the High/Scope Perry Pre-school study through age 27*. Michigan: High/Scope Press.

Schweinhart, L.J., Weikart, D. P. and Larner, M. B. (1986), 'Consequences of three pre-school curriculum models through age 15'. *Early Childhood Research Quarterly*, 1, 15–45.

Scott, S. (2000), 'The SPOKES project: supporting parents on kids education'. Paper presented at the National Family and Parenting Institute seminar on Promoting Positive Parenting. London.

Scott, S. and Sylva, K. (1999), 'Enabling parents'. Paper presented at the Department of Health Supporting Parents Initiative, Third Research Seminar. Egham, Surrey.

Smith, M. and Bissell, J. (1970), 'The impact of Head Start: the Westinghouse-Ohio Head Start evaluation'. *Harvard Educational Review*, 40, 51–104.

Statham, J. (1994), *Childcare in the community: the provision of community based, open access services for young children in family centres*. London: Save the Children Fund.

Stevenson, J., Sonuga-Barke, E. and Thompson, M. (1999), 'Strategies for parents with young children with behaviour problems'. Paper presented at the Department of Health Supporting Parents Initiative, Third Research Seminar. Egham, Surrey.

Sylva, K. and Hurry, J. (1995), *The effectiveness of reading recovery and phonological training for children with reading problems*. London: Thomas Coram Research Unit.

Sylva, K. and Wiltshire, J. (1993), 'The impact of early learning on children's later development: a review prepared for the inquiry 'Start Right'. *European Early Childhood Education Research Journal*, 1, 17–40.

Sylva, K., Siraj-Blatchford, I. and Johnson, S. (1992), 'The impact of the UK National Curriculum on preschool practice: some 'top down' processes at work'. *International Journal of Early Childhood*, 24, 41–51.

Sylva, K., Smith, T. and Moore, E. (1986), *Monitoring the High/Scope training programme – 1984–1985: final report*. Oxford: Department of Social and Administrative Studies, University of Oxford.

Tizard, J. and Hughes, M. (1984), *Young children learning*. London: Fontana.

Tizard, J., Schofield, W. and Hewison, J. (1982), 'Collaboration between teachers and parents in assisting children's reading'. *British Journal of Educational Psychology*, 52, 1–15.

Utting, D. (1995), *Family and parenthood: supporting families, preventing breakdown*. York: Joseph Rowntree Foundation.

— (1996), *Reducing criminality among young people: a sample of relevant programmes in the UK*. Home Office Research Study 161. London: Home Office.

Webster-Stratton, C. (1994), 'Randomized trial of two-parent training programmes for families with conduct-disordered children'. *Journal of Consulting and Clinical Psychology*, 52, 666–678.

— (1998), 'Parent-training with low income families'. In J. R. Lutzker (ed.), *Handbook of child abuse research and treatment*. New York: Plenum Press.

Welsh, B. (1997), *Costs and benefits of primary prevention: a review of the literature*. Paper presented at the High Security Psychiatric Services Commissioning Board (Department of Health) conference on Primary Prevention of Adult Antisocial Behaviour. London.

Westinghouse Learning Corporation (1969), *The impact of Head Start: an evaluation of the effects of Head Start on children's cognitive and affective development.* Report to the Office of Economic Opportunity. Washington, DC: Clearing House for Federal, Scientific and Technical Information.

Woodhead, M. (1985), 'Pre-school education has long term effects: but can they be generalized'? *Oxford Review of Education*, 11, 133–155.

Zoritch, B., Roberts, I. and Oakley, A. (1998), 'The health and welfare effects of daycare: a systematic review of randomised controlled trials'. *Social Science and Medicine*, 47, 317–327.

# Appendix

## SOCIAL SUPPORT AND PREGNANCY OUTCOME (SSPO)
(Oakley, Rajan and Grant, 1990; Oakley, 1992)

Location: 4 UK Hospitals
Type: Randomized Control Trial

### TARGET GROUPS
The target group of pregnant women (N=509) all had a history of low birth weight (<2,500 g) and the sample was predominantly socially disadvantaged: 77 per cent were working class, 18 per cent had unemployed partners and 41 per cent were smoking at booking.

### PROJECT DESCRIPTION
There was random allocation to the intervention group, who were provided with social support in the form of visits (a minimum of 3) and 24 hour telephone support by specially selected and trained midwives. During the visit the midwives provided a listening service, gave practical information and advice when asked, carried out referrals and collected information. Seventy per cent received more than the minimum package. The control group had traditional care.

### OUTCOMES
*Pregnancy and birth*: the average birth weight was increased and the likelihood of very low weight babies was decreased, as were the amount of hospital admissions and the overall level of obstetric complications and interventions.

*First few weeks*: mothers and babies were healthier as judged by self-report and use of health services. Attitudes towards the intervention were positive, and it was felt that the most important aspect of the intervention was that the midwife had listened. Working-class women also particularly valued the advice element. Most of the mothers considered the research midwife was helpful.

## DISCUSSION

The women were disadvantaged in both obstetric and social terms. The intervention was delivered as planned to the vast majority of the original sample, but one consequence of the method of recruitment was that some mothers in the control group also perceived an increase in support.

The increase in mean birth weight was in the direction hypothesised but was not significant (a larger sample size would have been required). The authors suggest that intervention effects were most evident in the area of medical care, in that less obtrusive medical care was required for mothers or babies. The improved emotional well-being of the socially supported mothers was felt to be an effect which would continue to be helpful for the babies.

Oakley and colleagues say, 'in the direction of promoting continuity of care and a less impersonal and a more sensitive antenatal service, it is important to remember that social policy changes are also needed to improve the health-denying conditions in which many mothers and babies live.' (Oakley, Rajan and Grant, 1990).

Although the mothers valued the listening aspect of the intervention there were other important dimensions: the intervention was delivered in their own home, it could be initiated or controlled by mother, it provided listening, was non-judgmental, and sympathetic practical advice was offered, as well as appropriate referral to both health and welfare agencies.


## THE COMMUNITY MOTHERS PROGRAMME

(Johnson, Howell and Molloy, 1993; Johnson and Molloy, 1995)

Location: Dublin, Ireland
Type: Randomized Control Trial

*TARGET GROUPS*

Selection was first made of disadvantaged/deprived areas which had large numbers of births. The criteria for area selection included housing type, social class, education and unemployment, as derived from census and other data. The major target group was 262 first-time mothers who were delivered in a six-month period during 1989. The second group was 30 experienced mothers from the same community, who were recruited by a combination of local knowledge, snowball, and cascade effect (i.e. mothers who had previously been recipients of this intervention).


*PROJECT DESCRIPTION*

A project structure involved a number of programme co-ordinators or Family Development Nurses who were each responsible for recruiting and supporting up to 20 'community mothers' at any one time. These mothers were expected to have a caring sensitive nature, reasonable literacy and an interest in the community; and were trained over approximately 6 hours in their own home. Each of the 'community mothers' was in turn responsible for 5–15 first-time mothers who were allocated to them or a control group at random. The community mothers visited the target mothers at least monthly for the first year of the child's life and provided a long visit discussing the child's development and the mothers input in a way tailored to individual family circumstances. The control group received standard support from the public health nurse.

*OUTCOMES*

A large proportion (89 per cent) of the first-time mothers completed the study. Baseline demographic data was collected at first interview and a questionnaire administered on the child's first birthday.

Study or intervention children were more likely to have received all of their primary immunisations, to have been read to, and read to daily, to have played more cognitive games and have been exposed to more nursery rhymes. Their weaning and diet was judged to be more appropriate.

Mothers in the 'community mothers' group also reported a better diet and at the end of the study, were less likely to report being tired, feeling miserable or wanting to stay indoors. They reported more positive feelings and fewer negative feelings. There were no differences between intervention and control groups on hospital admissions. It should, however, be noted that these outcome assessments were not made blind to group allocation.

*DISCUSSION*

This programme was not delivered by professionals but by experienced mothers living in the same communities. These mothers were expected to share experiences and raise self-esteem and confidence in parenting (which could be seen as social support). These results are seen to support a model of empowerment, and to be sound, practical and effective.

## PERRY PRE-SCHOOL PROJECT – HIGH/SCOPE EDUCATION

(Schweinhart and Weikart, 1980; Berrueta-Clement et al., 1984; Schweinhart, Weikart and Larner, 1986; Schweinhart, Barnes and Weikart, 1993)

Location: Ypsilanti, Michigan, USA
Type: Randomized Control Trial

*TARGET GROUP*
African-American pre-schoolers aged 3–4 years, from low-income families, and who were at risk of school failure and intellectual retardation/ IQ less than 90, were recruited in 4 cohorts (1962–1965), (N=123).

*PROJECT DESCRIPTION*
Over 2 years – $2^1/_2$ hours, 5 days a week of intensive academic stimulation with the High/Scope Curriculum which was organized on Piagetian principles of child-initiated learning, direct experiences with hands on materials, and a 'plan-do-review' cycle for conducting activities, which were a mixture of physical, social, and intellectual tasks. Children were actively involved in making choices about their activities. Emphasis was on small groups and a high child–staff ratio (5–6 children per teacher) and a high quality curriculum. Parents were involved: there were home visits by teachers (of about 90 minutes' duration) and also in active participation in monthly small groups.

## OUTCOMES

*Up to age 19:*
- better academic achievement
- graduation rates higher
- employment levels higher
- lower arrest rates
- charged with less serious crimes
- fewer pregnancies and births
- fewer on welfare

*age 27:*
- above results confirmed
- large differences in several measures of criminal activity
- higher home ownership, and fewer on welfare
- mean length of marriage longer

## DISCUSSION

Although there were no cognitive differences at middle school age, it is generally accepted that the long-term benefits resulted from a high quality programmme for all participants – children, teachers and parents. It is not always clear which elements in the programme were effective and brought about the long-term benefits. Most discussion of the better long-term outcomes for Perry Pre-Schoolers has focused on the curriculum inputs (High/Scope) but it is also possible that the effects, or some of them, were due to reduction in grade retention, working to increase self-esteem. The true nature of the random allocation was questioned by Farran (1990).

This study has been influential because of the long-term evaluation and the cost benefit analysis, where it has been estimated that for every dollar invested $7 were yielded in return.

## READING RECOVERY (ENGLISH EVALUATION)
(Sylva and Hurry, 1995; Hurry and Sylva, 1997)

Location: London and South East, UK
Type: Partial Random Control Trial

*TARGET GROUP*
Young children with marked reading difficulties identified after at least 1 year full-time primary school education; bottom 20 per cent, N= 390 (1992), N=342 (1996).

*PROJECT DESCRIPTION*
The sample comprised six children from each of 63 schools, mainly in inner-city areas, who were the poorest readers on the basis of a battery of reading assessments administered at age $6-6^1/_2$ years. The children were randomly allocated either to the Reading Recovery (RR) condition, or to the phonological condition. In control schools the six poorest readers, identified as above, were all assigned to the control group.

The effects of the two interventions were assessed by a within-school comparison and an across-condition (or schools) comparison. The children were tested prior to the intervention, immediately afterwards and at two further points by a 'blind' evaluator. The aim was to evaluate two programmes, RR and a phonological intervention, and to compare the outcomes with the 'usual' levels of school support for poor readers.

*Interventions* (1) RR: $^1/_2$ hour a day (i.e. $2^1/_2$ hours a week) up to 20 weeks by trained teacher using levelled books including a phonological element. (2) Phonological: 40, 10-minute sessions with a trained teacher.

*OUTCOMES*

At the onset of the study many of the children could barely read, but on average the children who received either intervention were doing slightly worse than the control group, and therefore comparisons took account of initial ability using regression analysis. At first follow up the RR children had made substantially more progress than controls on all measures of reading and writing. Children in the phonological intervention group were ahead on phonological awareness. A year later children in the RR condition were still showing benefits in reading, spelling, and phonological awareness compared with similar children in other schools, but the gap had narrowed. At the end of primary school the differences between children in both intervention groups and controls were no longer significant. However, for the smaller group of more disadvantaged children in the sample (identified as those taking free school meals), the significant effects of RR were maintained at the longer term follow-up. The phonological intervention was also effective for socially disadvantaged children. If the analysis was concentrated on the very poorest readers, RR was more effective than the phonological intervention. The phonological intervention, on the other hand, seemed to be more effective in teaching those who initially had slightly better reading skills.

*DISCUSSION*

Both interventions (RR more strongly) showed intervention effects which faded with time, but for the most disadvantaged children, both socially and in initial reading readiness it continued to compensate. In terms of cost effectiveness, Hurry and Sylva say, 'Although, in the short-term RR was a costly intervention, in the longer term it seems unlikely that it is substantially more costly than educating any child with reading difficulties'.

## NEWPIN (NEW PARENT INFANT NETWORK)

(Cox et al., 1991; Oakley et al., 1995)

Location: 4 family centres London, UK
Type: Outcome evaluation

*TARGET GROUPS*

The target population was vulnerable women under stress, and where there was danger of family breakdown. At the time of the evaluation (Oakley et al., 1995), there was a lack of clarity on whether the target group was mothers with depression, social isolation and poverty, or those with problems in areas of child rearing or abuse, but a reply from NEWPIN emphasized the former remit.

*PROJECT DESCRIPTION*

The intervention package was a mix of social involvement, therapy and training. The evaluation found that most clients were referred by Health Visitors, some by social workers and a few were self-referred. Most were single mothers with one or two children, half in their 20s, and two-thirds were white. The intervention involved for each referred mother: (i) an introductory chat; (ii) match with volunteer 'befriender'; (iii) a drop-in centre and a crèche, and (iv) encouragement to participate in training such as a personal development programme. The emphasis was on a caring community model involving a non hierarchical style of support.

*OUTCOMES*

A previous evaluation (Cox et al., 1991) had suggested that, although many referred mothers had benefited, 7–12 months of sustained involvement may be necessary for there to be significant improvement in the mothers' psychiatric state. The 1995 evaluation investigated 214 referrals made in 1992, to four centres in London. The response rate to a questionnaire was 63 per cent, which was described as a 'reasonable response for a population of high social disadvantage'. Those who completed the questionnaire were less disadvantaged and more likely to use the service.

The most common problems reported were social isolation or depression, followed by partner relationships, problems with children's behaviour or health, and problems about housing. Less than half of those surveyed had made any use of NEWPIN, and the majority of users went less than 5 times, that is, a large proportion of referrals did not become regular users of the service. Asked if it had helped, 47 per cent reported that it was quite or very helpful. Non-users said it did not meet needs or address their problems. Most of the small proportion who used the personal development programme said it had been useful. What those who did use NEWPIN reported that they most valued was the opportunity to meet other women.

*DISCUSSION*

NEWPIN did provide a valued service to a proportion of a very high-risk group. However, the proportion using and valuing the service were only a minority of those referred. Oakley wondered what happened to the referrals who did not go on to use the service, and commented that 'significant problems must be addressed in the interface between the voluntary and statutory sectors in family support'.

Comment on this evaluation (Buttigieg, 1995) stressed the importance of long-term effects and the difficulty of evaluation techniques with this disturbed group.